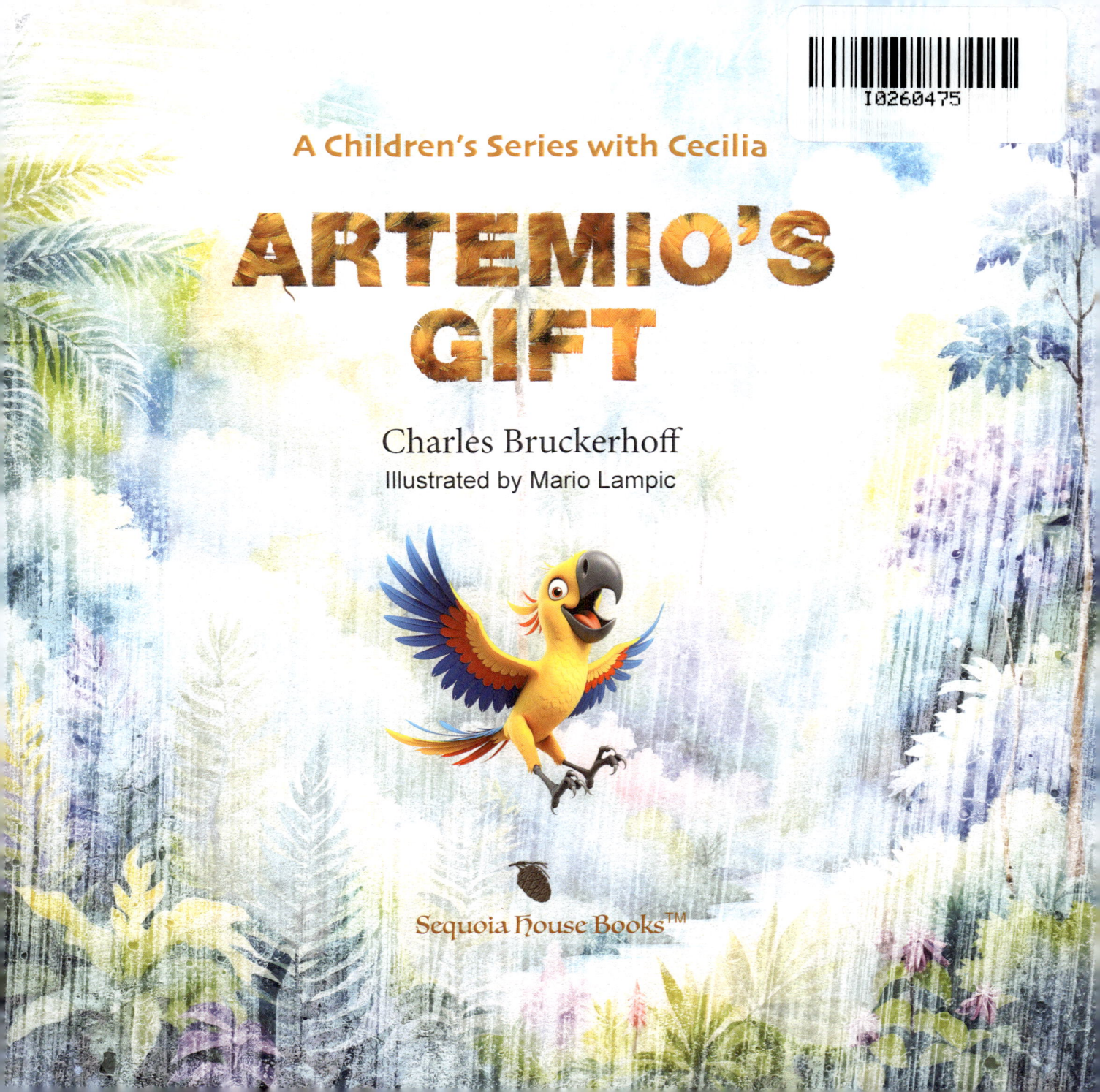

A Children's Series with Cecilia

ARTEMIO'S GIFT

Charles Bruckerhoff

Illustrated by Mario Lampic

Sequoia House Books™

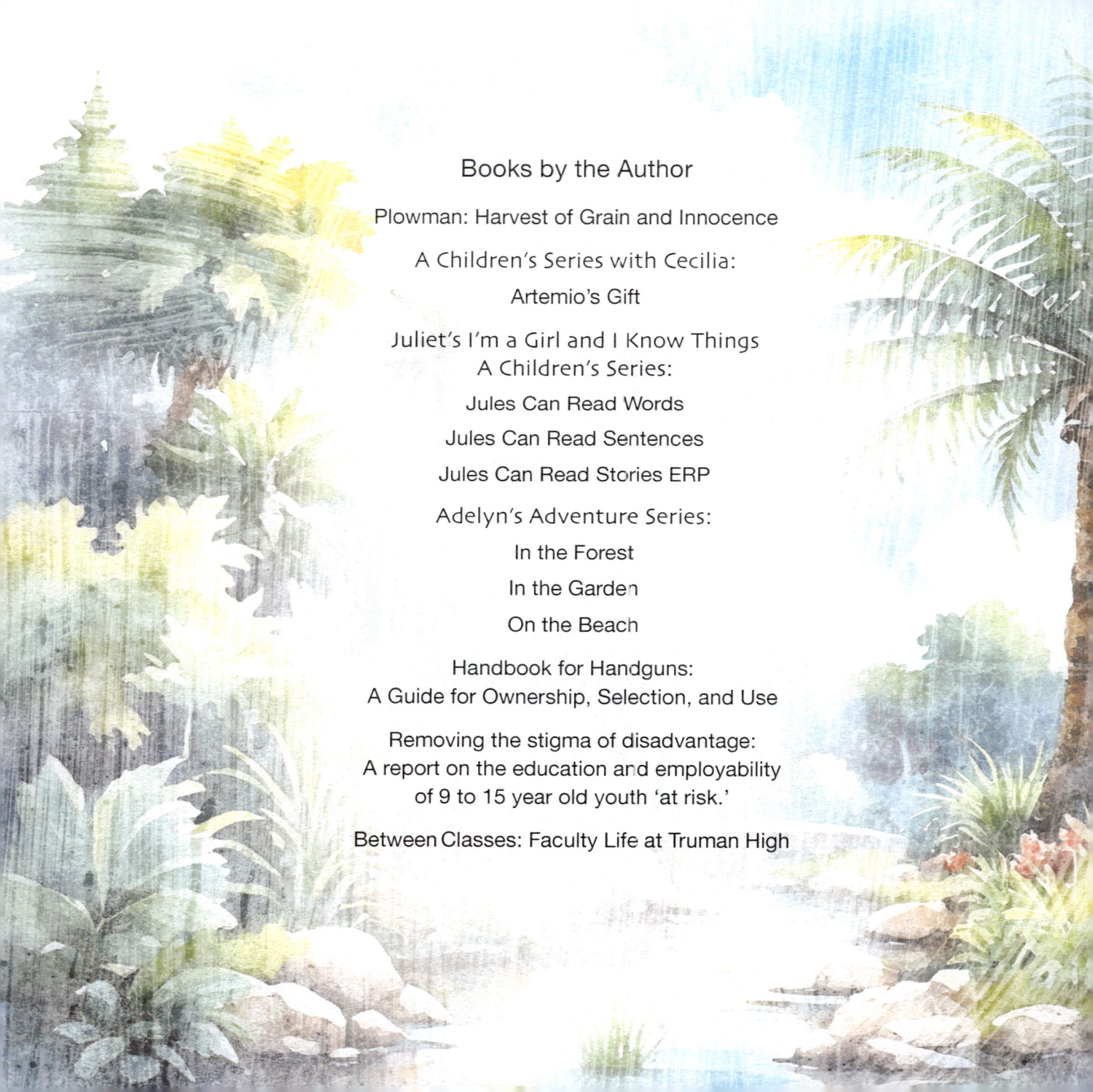

Books by the Author

Plowman: Harvest of Grain and Innocence

A Children's Series with Cecilia:
Artemio's Gift

Juliet's I'm a Girl and I Know Things
A Children's Series:
Jules Can Read Words
Jules Can Read Sentences
Jules Can Read Stories ERP

Adelyn's Adventure Series:
In the Forest
In the Garden
On the Beach

Handbook for Handguns:
A Guide for Ownership, Selection, and Use

Removing the stigma of disadvantage:
A report on the education and employability
of 9 to 15 year old youth 'at risk.'

Between Classes: Faculty Life at Truman High

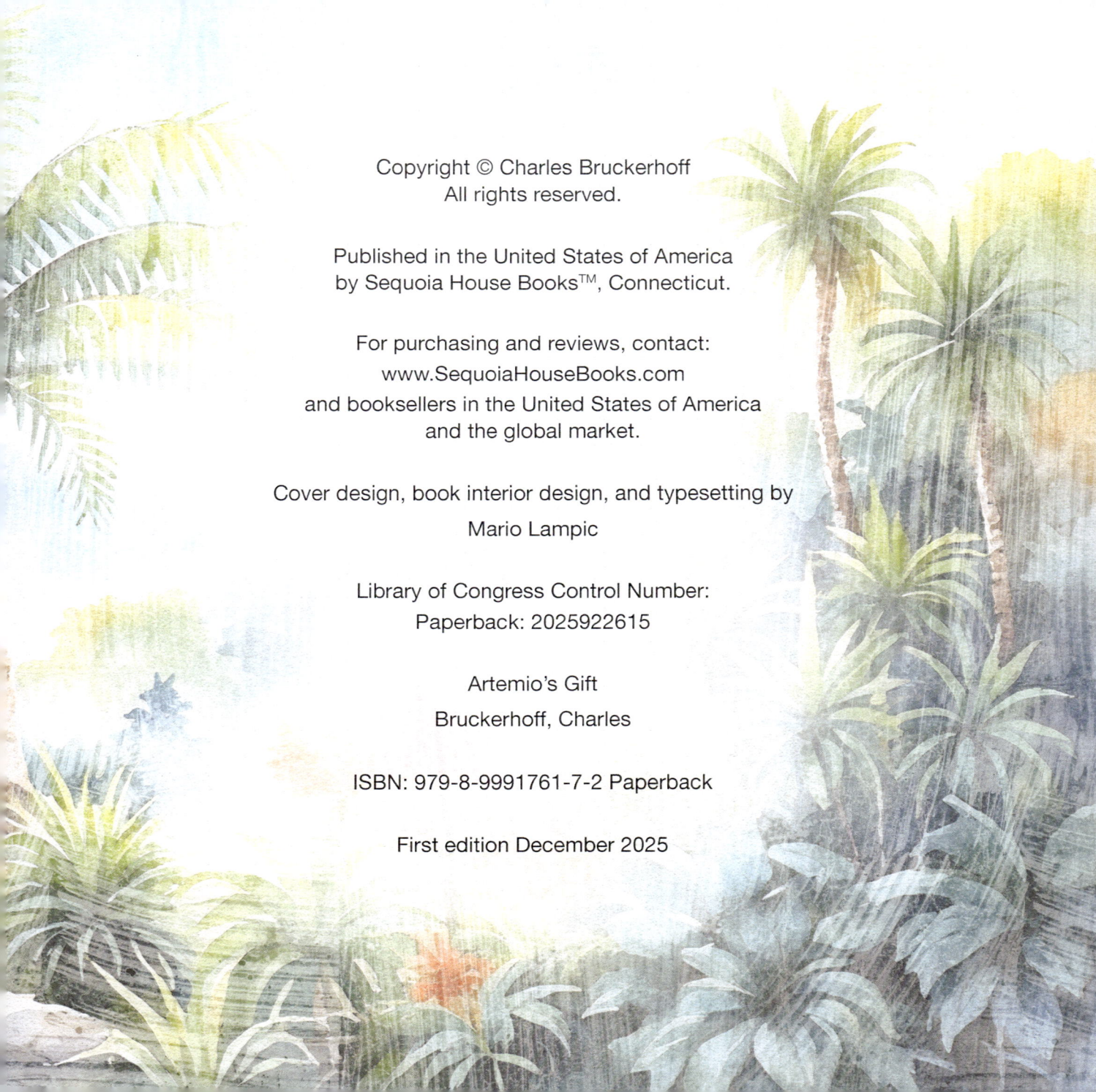

Copyright © Charles Bruckerhoff
All rights reserved.

Published in the United States of America
by Sequoia House Books™, Connecticut.

For purchasing and reviews, contact:
www.SequoiaHouseBooks.com
and booksellers in the United States of America
and the global market.

Cover design, book interior design, and typesetting by
Mario Lampic

Library of Congress Control Number:
Paperback: 2025922615

Artemio's Gift
Bruckerhoff, Charles

ISBN: 979-8-9991761-7-2 Paperback

First edition December 2025

Since it is so likely that children will meet cruel enemies, let them at least have heard of brave knights and heroic courage.

— C.S. Lewis

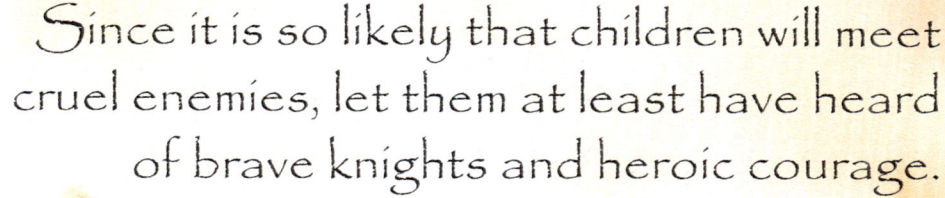

Cecilia Can Read

I can read words and sentences.

Now, I want to read stories.

Listen to me read **Artemio's Gift** to you.

One sunny April morning after breakfast, Viola helped Daddy rake the leaves, dead grass, and dry sticks into a big pile in the front yard.

They did the same work in the backyard.

They paused for lunch at noon.

Viola had a peanut butter and grape jelly sandwich, a bowl of Greek yogurt, and a glass of apple juice.

Daddy ate a hot roast beef sandwich with gravy, a large Pennsylvania Dutch soft pretzel, and a glass of water.

After lunch, Viola helped Daddy gather all the leaves, grass snippets, and sticks onto a tarp in the front yard. Then they pulled the tarp into the backyard and placed all the dry stuff on it as well.

Before dinnertime, they shoveled all the dried leaves, sticks, and grass clippings into the backyard waste barrel.

Daddy explained to Viola that over the next few winters, the waste barrel will turn those dead leaves, sticks, and grass clippings into new, rich soil for the vegetable and flower gardens.

Now the day's work was finished.

On their way back to the house, Viola noticed her clothes were soaked with sweat. The cool spring evening breeze was blowing gently, making her shiver. She wanted to warm up quickly.

Momma prepared Viola's favorite dinner: homemade chicken soup with dumplings, served with a strawberry spinach salad with toasted pecans, goat cheese, and apple cider vinaigrette. For dessert, she baked chocolate-pecan cupcakes topped with a creamy frosting. Viola also had a glass of milk.

"Momma, dinner was so good! And really warmed me up," Viola said with a wide yawn.

Momma said, "You and Daddy worked so hard outside all day. That's why we ate a late dinner. Viola, you look so tired. Are you ready to go to bed?"

"Yeah," Viola said as she got up from her chair, took her bowl and cup to the sink, and went upstairs.

She bathed, brushed her teeth, and changed into her pajamas.

Viola sat drowsily on the edge of her bed, waiting for Daddy to read her a book about the dinosaurs that roamed the earth millions of years ago.

"The Illustrated Dinosaurs on Planet Earth" was a wordless picture book.

Viola could read chapter books on her own, but on nights when she was tired, she wanted Daddy to read her a story from her favorite dinosaur book.

This book had vivid, large, and delightful pictures. Viola was fascinated by the colorful drawings of the dinosaurs and the strange land where they lived.

When Daddy read to her, his voice was always full of excitement, as if it were their first time reading this story. As Daddy turned the pages, he talked about each dinosaur and pointed out its unique features.

The way he told the story made Viola believe they were really in the land of dinosaurs. She imagined real

dinosaurs roaming everywhere, looking for food and water. In her bedroom, her house, the front yard, and the backyard—all over, the neighborhood became a strange, wild land where dinosaurs roamed freely.

Daddy walked into her room and asked, "Are you ready for a story, Viola?"

"Oh yeah. Read my dinosaur book," she responded, yawning.

Daddy went to the bookcase and pulled out the dinosaur book. Then he sat on the edge of her bed beside her.

He opened "Dinosaurs on Planet Earth" to the first page and began telling the story.

"Some dinosaurs were enormous creatures, Viola. See here: taller than our house and taller than the trees on our street.

"They truly were incredible beings.

"And looking very strange.

"This one had a very long neck, a big body, and an extra-long tail.

"Nose to tail, it was as long as our street outside. You and your friends could take turns sliding down its neck and tail.

"The Brontosaurus!"

"Another one had three thick horns on its head, and its mouth was a bird-like beak. At the back of its head was a 'frill' resembling a hood

"This was the fierce-looking Triceratops!"

"Okay, Daddy. I'll turn the next page," Viola said.

"This dinosaur had wings that spread out to nearly twenty feet, longer than our living room. It could fly.

"Look at that! A dinosaur that soars high and low in the sky!

"With a long, skinny beak like a bird and a crest on its head, similar to our modern pileated woodpecker!

"The Pteranodon!"

"This page features a dinosaur that is very popular among kids today.

"See, it had a big head and a thick body! It stood twenty feet tall.

"That's taller than our house!

"It had many sharp teeth in its mouth.

"But look here, there are two small arms on its chest.

TYRANNOSAURUS REX

"It walked upright on these two enormous back legs.

"And here, check out its long, thick tail!

"This dinosaur is the one and only Tyrannosaurus Rex!

"Or just, T. rex."

Viola asked, "Daddy, did dinosaurs have friends? Did they play together outside?"

"We don't know because they lived on Earth so many, many years ago," Daddy said. "Everything we know about dinosaurs comes from piecing together their ancient bones, what they ate, and other clues found where they died so many millions of years ago.

"But, of course, you can imagine that the little ones sometimes play with each other.

"Nowadays, baby wild bears, baby wild monkeys, baby wild deer, baby wild horses, baby wild lions, and baby wild tigers play with each other and with their parents just like we do as a family. We do so at home, in the park, at the gym, and at the swimming pool."

Viola said dreamily, "I would like to have the pteranodon for my friend. We would fly around our neighborhood."

"Go visit my Grandma and Grandpa in the countryside, and my other grandparents in the city.

"We would do all kinds of things with you and Momma.

"Fly to the beach.

"Fly to the gym.

"Fly to my school.

"Fly to the ice cream parlor and buy some ice cream treats. I would order a strawberry ice cream cone.

"Fly back home again.

"I would show the pteranodon to all my aunts and uncles, my cousins at birthday parties and holidays, and to my friends on the street, the Uber drivers, my teachers, and our mailman."

They weren't even halfway through the storybook when Daddy gently closed the covers. Viola's eyes were closed, and her head was nodding.

She yawned loudly and widely.

Then, she laid on her back with her head on the pillow and said, "I love you, Daddy, and Momma, too. Good night."

Daddy kissed her cheek.

She closed her eyes.

Daddy pulled the covers up to her chin, turned off the lamp, left the room, and closed the door.

"Click."

Viola asked sleepily, "Oh, Daddy, leave the door open, please?"

"Sure, Viola," Daddy said as he cracked open the door.

Viola closed her eyes and drifted into a deep sleep.

A wondrous dream came to Viola — a dream unlike any other. It began with a strange sound drifting through her open bedroom window, carried by the dark nighttime air outside.

"hoo-h'HOO-hoo-hoo."

And the sound repeated, but it came from a different direction.

"hoo-h'HOO-hoo-hoo."

A few minutes later, she heard the sound again, but it was very close.

"hoo-h'HOO-hoo-hoo."

And again, from a different angle.

"hoo-h'HOO-hoo-hoo."

Viola was curious. She threw off the covers and went to her bedroom window. She opened it wide, eager to find out what was making that strange sound.

Then she heard a loud "whoosh" and saw the thick tree branch near her window bend way down. Something heavy had landed on it.

"hoo-h'HOO-hoo-hoo. Are you there, Viola?" a voice said.

That question took her by surprise.

"Yes. I'm here. And I'm looking out my window." Viola answered. "It's dark out there, and I don't see you, whoever you are."

The voice said, "We are your feathered friends. Open your window all the way and step back. We will come into your bedroom."

"Okay," Viola said. She stepped back and stood next to her dresser. Suddenly, two large gray birds flew into Viola's room. They perched together on the footboard of her bed.

Viola said, "You are giant birds! I mean ginormous birds! Taller than my baseball bat and as wide as my school backpack. What kind of birds are you?" she asked.

"We're Great Horned Owls," one of the birds said in a very dignified voice. "I'm Harriet. And this is my best friend and soul mate, Harold. We need your help, Viola," Harriet said.

Viola asked, "How can I help you?"

Then, in the dim light of her bedroom, Viola noticed that Harold's feet, wings, and body were tightly tangled in a green 6-inch mesh trellis netting, similar to what gardeners use to train flowers and vegetables to grow upward.

"Yeah, that's it. You found it," Harriet said when she saw Viola staring at the unnatural nylon twine netting wrapped around Harold's body.

"Yesterday, Harold was snatching up a field mouse for our dinner when he flew into the netting. He can't do much with that stuff wrapped around him. He can only fly short distances. He has a hard time eating.

It's cutting into his skin and making him bleed. We tried and tried to remove it, but with only our beaks and claws, we couldn't get it off. Can you please help us?" Harriet asked

"Let me take a closer look," Viola offered.

"Yeah, I think I can help you. I've got an idea. Stay there while I grab my scissors," Viola said. Viola walked to her dresser and opened the top drawer. She reached in, took out a pair of very sharp fabric scissors in a leather case, and went back to her bed.

The birds still perched on the footboard, but now they looked nervous. They shifted their perches, moving together in a dance-like manner, slowly stepping from right to left and then back again. Over and over.

Viola unzipped the leather case and pulled out the scissors.

"Hold still, both of you! Harold especially," Viola said sternly. "This operation shouldn't hurt at all, but my scissors are very sharp. Cutting the nylon string is tricky, and if I make a mistake, you could get badly hurt."

"Okay," the two owls said in unison.

"Snip."

"Snip."

"Snip."

"Oooo, this one is really tight, cutting into your skin," Viola said. "You're bleeding here. Hold still, especially, Harold."

"Snip. . . Snip. . . Snip. Okay, I got it!"

"Snip."

"Snip."

"Snip."

"There, at last. That was a messy, tangled disaster. I can't believe you managed anything with that netting wrapped around you.

"I got all of the string off your legs, feet, wings, and body, Harold," Viola said, relieved that her plan worked. She gathered the loose netting, bunching it into a tight ball, and tossed it into the wastebasket in the corner of her bedroom.

"How are you feeling now?" Viola asked.

"Great!"

Harold ruffled his feathers twice and jumped off the footboard. He flew up and down and all around her bedroom three times. He swooped low, grabbed Viola's pillow in his claws, fluffed it, and dropped it into her open arms.

Then he gently brushed both her cheeks with his feathery wing tips and said, "Thanks, Viola. I feel free again! I'm so relieved. Now I can help Harriet raise our new family," Harold said happily.

"Thank you, Viola!" Harriet exclaimed. "We were so worried about the worst—that Harold might die."

"I'm glad I could help you," Viola said. "But I can't tell which one of you is Harriet and which one is Harold. You both look and sound the same to me. Wait a minute. I've got an idea. Harriet, that's you on the right?" Viola asked while pointing to her.

"Yeah, yesterday, today, and, Lord willing, tomorrow," Harriet answered with a laugh. "I am right here, Harriet, standing tall and proud, always."

Viola said, "Don't move. Give me one second." She returned to her dresser and opened the bottom drawer. This time, she grabbed a 6-pack of fancy nail polish that Grandma had given her.

Viola said, "Hope you don't mind, but this fingernail paint will help me know who's speaking to me."

Viola painted each of Harriet's claws with "Ruby Red with Sprinkles" nail polish.

Then, she picked up another nail polish, "Blue Jelly with Sprinkles," and applied it to Harold's claws.

"Shazam! Now I'll know who's talking to me and who I'm talking to!" Viola said, laughing.

Both owls looked down in total amazement at their brightly painted claws.

"hoo-h'HOO-hoo-hoo, it looks magnificent!" hooted Harriet.

"hoo-h'HOO-hoo-hoo, and so classy!" Harold hooted.

But Viola was puzzled. "I'm looking at your legs and feet, and they have scales on them. Good grief! I didn't know birds had scales on their feet and legs. I thought only reptiles had scales—like lizards, snakes, Komodo dragons, alligators, geckos, iguanas, turtles, and crocodiles!"

"Oh yeah," Harold said. "That's true about those reptiles, but we birds have scales too. In fact, we descend from theropod dinosaurs, including the big one, Tyrannosaurus Rex. They were reptiles—had scales, laid eggs, and some even had wings so they could fly. We have wings, and we fly. We reproduce offspring in eggs. We have scales on our legs and feet. Truth be told, we have some pretty cool ancestors, too, Viola!"

"Are you reading about dinosaurs?" Harriet asked while nodding toward the book on the nightstand that Daddy had read to Viola earlier.

"Yeah, I love learning about dinosaurs. I wish I could see them in the land where they lived," Viola said. "But I can't. Daddy said they roamed the earth millions of years ago and are now extinct. That's so sad."

"Harriet," Harold asked, "is there enough time for your eggs to develop before we need to sit on the nest and hatch our new brood?"

"Yeah, I think we have a few days. Why?" Harriet asked.

Harold said, "We should thank Viola for helping get that nasty netting off my body. We can take her on a little trip back in time to our secret hideout."

"Great idea, Harold. We can definitely do that," Harriet said.

"Viola, are you ready for an adventure?" Harold asked.

Viola replied, "I would love to. But how? And where?"

"Grab what you want to take with you, we're heading out now," Harold said.

Viola put the leather case with the scissors and the six-pack of nail polish in the pocket of her pajamas.

She shouted, "I'm ready!"

Harold pointed out the window with his wing, "Viola, Solomon the Great One is waiting for you. Climb onto his neck and hang on tight. We will guide both of you."

Solomon was standing on the roof above the kitchen, outside her window. Viola shouted, "You're a huge owl, twice the size of Daddy!"

She climbed onto Solomon's shoulders, hugged his neck tightly, and grasped the deep, soft feathers with her fingers.

Instinctively, Harold and Harriet jumped out the window and hovered above Viola and Solomon. Then all three owls flapped their wings vigorously. Minutes later, they soared high in the sky.

Viola couldn't believe what just happened.

One moment, she was applying glittery nail polish to the owls' claws to tell them apart. The next, she was soaring high and fast under the moon, stars, and planets, carried by Solomon the

Great One and guided by Harriet and Harold—three majestic horned owls.

Viola was on an adventure with the owls, but where was their secret hideout?

She looked down and saw the signs, roads, and streetlights—her home, her neighborhood, and all the buildings of her town she knew so well.

A police car, with its lights flashing and siren blaring, was chasing a speeding red vehicle. An ambulance with flashing lights and a wailing siren was rushing to Mercy Hospital with someone who was sick or injured. Soon enough, all the noise and activity from her town fell silent.

They were high above, and her house, yard, neighborhood, and town disappeared below.

The owls were flying very fast and high. She looked up and around, marveling at what she saw.

Viola said, "The stars are shining everywhere — so clear, so bright, and twinkling."

"And the planets are shining their light so bright and steady!

"There's the Big Dipper! . . . And the North Star!

"The Moon! . . . our planet Earth! . . . Mercury! . . . Venus! . . . Mars! . . . Jupiter! . . . Saturn! . . . Uranus! . . .

and Neptune! . . . And all the millions upon millions of stars in the Milky Way. There it is! I see the Milky Way!"

A gentle breeze tousled Viola's hair. She felt dizzy for the first time in her life.

The day's yard work outside and the warm chicken soup with dumplings for dinner made Viola very tired. She rested her head on the soft feathers of Solomon's neck and relaxed.

The three owls continued flying away with Viola resting on Solomon's neck. They traveled to a faraway place and to a long-forgotten time.

When Viola woke up, the sun was rising over the horizon. It was a new morning in a new place.

Viola turned over, sat up, and realized she had been sleeping on the ground. Her bed was made from tall, soft, bent grasses. She looked around and saw that she was sitting high on a mountainside at the edge of a cliff.

Solomon, Harold, and Harriet sat high above her on a thick tree limb.

"You are in a different time and place now, Viola," Harriet said. "A new adventure awaits you. Enjoy it. We will always be here watching over you."

Harold said, "When your adventure ends, we will take you back home."

Solomon shouted, "Now have fun!"

Viola saw the "Ruby Red with Sprinkles" and the "Blue Jelly with Sprinkles" nail polish shining on Harriet's and Harold's claws. She also saw the tall, handsome, wise Solomon. That made her feel safe.

5

"Where am I?" Viola asked herself.

She stood and looked around. In the distance, she saw a huge mountain with an active volcano, spewing gray and black clouds, hot dark ash, fiery sparks, and red-hot molten lava. The red lava flowed down the mountain like a raging river of fire, steaming, spitting, oozing, and splattering until it reached the cold ocean, where waves crashed onto a white sandy beach.

The forests surrounding her had gigantic trees, much taller than any Viola had ever seen. Tall green reeds grew along the edge of a sparkling, clear lake nearby. They stood straight and stiff, with long, narrow leaves and bright red flowers at the top.

Dead, decaying leaves, sticks, grasses, reeds, limbs, vines, and logs lay in huge, chaotic piles everywhere.

"Nothing here is raked clean or stacked in tidy piles. You brought me to a wild hideout, Owls!" Viola remarked.

The sun shone brightly, and fluffy white clouds drifted across the blue

sky. Then a strong, gusty wind blew gray and black clouds across the sky, blocking out the sun and making the day nearly as dark as night.

"A rainstorm is coming!" Viola shouted.

Horrific lightning struck the earth many times, and thunder shook the ground and rumbled through the air. Then the dark clouds sent down thick sheets of rain, pouring tons of water onto the land.

The rain drenched Viola's hair and pajamas. She shivered briefly.

As quickly as the storm arrived, it also passed. Then the sun shined in a clear, blue sky. The air warmed up again. Steam rose everywhere from the rain-soaked hills, forests, and meadows.

Viola saw a long line of big, brown, weird-looking creatures crawling across the ground toward her.

"They look like some kind of insect," Viola guessed.

They hurried toward her, cranky. They moved on six, angled, skinny legs. On the fronts of their heads, they had two rounded, glaring black eyes. Two long antennas protruded from their beady, brown heads. These ugly-looking creatures were constantly swirling the whippy antennas on their heads, trying to sense what was nearby.

When they suddenly came across a puddle of water, the entire swarm flexed their wings to fly over it.

"Cockroaches!" Viola yelled. "A bunch of gross cockroaches!" She remembered the day when Momma and Grandma found a bunch of them hiding under a wet newspaper in the garage. They quickly squished all the cockroaches.

But the cockroaches Viola saw now running toward her in this strange land were much larger. They were longer, wider, and taller than Daddy's shoes! And they looked mean, hungry, and vicious.

Viola moved aside from their path but kept watching their movements.

Then she heard thunderous footsteps that shook the ground beneath her.

"Thud!"

"Thud!"

"Thud!"

"Thud!"

"Thud!"

"That is one huge creature, and it's definitely moving closer to me," Viola said to herself.

While Viola was distracted, a large, bird-like creature silently landed on the edge of the cliff. It approached Viola and stood directly behind her. The bird used its long beak to peck at Viola's shoulder to draw her attention.

"Ms. Viola?" the bird squawked.

Looking up, Viola yelled, "Hey, you're a pteranodon!"

"Yeah, my friends call me Don the Pteranodon, or just Don."

Then Don politely bowed to Viola.

"Nice to meet you, Ms. Viola.

"We have places to go, things to see, and stuff to do. We can't afford to waste time. I'm so glad it's early morning. We need the whole day.

"And a Tyrannosaurus Rex is rushing in from right over there!"

Don asked, "Will you come with me, Ms. Viola?"

"Yeah, but where are we going? How are we going to get there? And how will we get back here safely?" Viola asked.

"Oh, by the way, Don the Pteranodon, please call me Viola," she said, laughing.

"Okay, Viola, it is," Don answered. "I'm taking you deep into the primeval forest where all the dinosaurs roam. We have no time to waste. T. rex will be here any minute now. But I promised Harriet, Harold, and

Solomon—your owl friends sitting on that limb—that I would bring you back here safe and sound before sunset today.

"Climb on my back, Viola. This bird is about to fly away now!"

Viola planted her foot on Don's short, outstretched leg. She pulled herself up to sit on his back and wrapped her arms tightly around his neck.

Don jumped up, flapped his monster wings, ran to the edge of the cliff, and shouted, "Hang on, Viola! Here we go!"

Don leaped off the high cliff edge. They fell quickly

into the hot jungle air. Don beat his wings smoothly. Soon, they were gliding swiftly over the treetops. With the rising air from the scorching sun and the steam from the rainstorm, they climbed higher and higher above the forest.

    They careened left and right, shooting down the steep mountainside. Flew back and forth, whirling spectacularly again and again, higher than lower, then higher than lower. "Don, this feels like I'm riding a wild rollercoaster!"

    Don swooped low to glide over the cresting blue waves of a large lake.

Then they flew into a stunning valley.

Don's wing tips and Viola's feet brushed against the tops of reeds, flowers, bushes, and shrubs.

Minutes later, they soared above a deep canyon with a raging river below. Don's flight dipped just above the turbulent whitewater and cut through the spray, splashing wildly all around them. They glided out of the canyon and over the treetops of a lush, primeval forest.

This was a land that no one but Viola had ever seen.

Now, Don circled over a wide, peaceful meadow. Viola watched a herd of duck-billed dinosaurs, hadrosaurs, grazing in the weeds near the edge of a forest.

At the other end of the meadow, a herd of stegosaurs grazed on grass, weeds, brush, low-hanging fruits,

and leaves, with some being big and old, some much younger, and some just babies.

A massive brontosaurus with a small head at the end of a long neck stood among the stegosaur herd. It was browsing and munching on leaves, branches, and fruits high above the ground. The giant brontosaurus could feed on foods like fruits, vegetables, leaves, and twigs that shorter dinosaurs couldn't reach.

Three ankylosaurs were feeding on ferns and shrubs across the meadow. Their sharp, thick, spiny plates kept away any creatures that might try to eat them for lunch.

Viola saw tree limbs breaking and leaves flying through the air on one side of the meadow. Tyrannosaurus Rex was there, thrashing its head wildly, clearing trees and brush to eat the body of a dead brontosaurus it had killed.

"Viola, look over there on our right!" Don suddenly shouted. They had just flown out of the forest, and now they were gliding over a wide bay at the edge of an ocean.

Don told Viola to watch as a giant plesiosaur surfaced and dove repeatedly, swallowing a large school of fish.

The shallow water in the bay was stained red with the blood of hundreds of fish the plesiosaur was eating.

"How are you enjoying the ride so far, Viola?" Don asked.

"Fantastic," Viola said. "So many amazing creatures live here! But it's so brutal! Your world is dangerous! All the animals I see are fighting for food, and they're either fighting or running from other dinosaurs that want to eat them. How do you survive?"

"That's life as I know it," Don said.

Don warned, "Viola, we need to take a break now because another rainstorm is heading our way from the ocean. You can see the dark clouds out there to our left with fierce lightning, thunder, rain, and hail pounding the land."

"Oh yeah. I see it!" Viola yelled over the raging, fast-moving storm.

She clung to Don's neck even tighter.

When Don first saw the storm heading toward land, he looked into the distance and picked a large cave on a seaside cliff for their safety.

Now he glided smoothly into the entrance and landed with a big bounce on the soft sandy floor.

"We'll wait out the storm here, Viola, then head to meet Harriet, Harold, and Solomon earlier than planned.

"Hop off and stretch your legs for a moment."

Viola was eager to do just that. The long flight was enjoyable, but her legs and arms

grew stiff from the constant bouncing and holding tightly onto Don's neck to avoid falling off.

Outside the cave, the storm raged fiercely. Lightning flashed white-hot, and thunder boomed

powerfully. The wind howled wildly, and rain poured down in sheets, blurring visibility. Hail fell from the sky, varying in size from grapes to grapefruits. It shattered tree limbs, grasses, and reeds, and stripped leaves and twigs from every plant in the valley. The ground was thickly covered everywhere with frozen balls of icy hail.

"That's one intense storm," Viola remarked.

"You betcha," Don said. "I didn't want us flying in that tempest. Harriet, Harold, and Solomon would disapprove! They would never trust me again. And besides, until the storm passes, it's too dark to fly."

"Hey, Don the Pteranodon," Viola said, giggling, "I'm going to paint your claws, your 'unguals.'"

"What?" Don asked, completely baffled.

"Wait and see," Viola said. She pulled the 6-pack of nail polish from her pajama pocket, opened the cap, and chose "Phosphorescent Green with Sprinkles."

"Don, when I finish painting your claws, you'll look like a tricked-out Halley's Comet streaking across the night sky."

"Halley's Comet. That's what I saw blazing through the dark nighttime sky last year, right on schedule again," Don said.

"Hold still," Viola said.

"Okay, whatever you say," Don replied, as he craned his neck to watch Viola's handiwork.

Viola stepped back to examine Don's feet and wings and to figure out the best way to paint Don's claws.

She shouted, "You have a lot of claws to paint. So spread out your wings and feet, Don!"

"Feet first!" she directed. "Lean over so I can do this for you," Viola said.

Don carefully followed Viola's instructions. She gently applied the "Phosphorescent Green with Sprinkles" nail polish to the five claws on Don's left foot. Then Viola had Don lean the other way to paint the five claws on his right foot.

Viola paused and took a step back to watch him.

"Don, what do you think?"

"Holy moly guacamole, Viola! My claws are glow-in-the-dark loud. I mean, really loud! Screaming loudly! Stupendous! Bodacious as that volcano!"

"Alright, Don, now bring down your wings one at a time so I can paint the claws on them," Viola directed.

Don lowered his left wing so Viola could paint all the claws, including the very long fourth claw.

"Wow, Don, that's a huge claw!

"Okay. Ready for your right wing, Don?" Viola asked.

Don turned his right side toward Viola and lowered that arm so she could apply the glittery nail polish.

When Viola finished with all his claws, she asked, "Don, do you wanna step out in a really bold way to impress your buddies?"

Viola laughed loudly, spun into a pirouette, bowed, and held out a new vial of fingernail polish. "Tada!" she exclaimed.

"I am not sure what you mean, Viola," Don said.

"Don, lower your head and close your eyes," Viola instructed. In her hand, she held the "Phosphorescent Red with Sprinkles" nail polish, and she applied it generously to Don's long beak.

Then she exclaimed, "Crazy loud! Don, you are one fabulous pteranodon! Open your eyes."

Don opened his eyes. He could only see the tip of his beak. But now his beak was shining "Phosphorescent Red with Sprinkles!"

"Goodness, what will my friends call me now?" Don wondered.

Viola predicted, "Don, you are the coolest, most fabulous, absolutely amazing glow-in-the-dark geeky pteranodon!"

Don said, "Viola, the rain has stopped. I'm going out for a test flight to see what I look like in the dark before the sun comes out again. Maybe my friends will see me."

In the next instant, Don leapt off the cliff, fell, and glided smoothly into the dark sky.

"Wow!" Viola shouted as she watched Don fly into the dark sky. "Don, you are one lit-up Haley's Comet for certain! Holy moly! You're spectacular."

"Grrrrrr! . . . Grrrrrr!" A loud growl came from deep inside the cave.

Viola turned around and listened as quiet footsteps slowly approached from the direction of the growl.

She stood completely still, looking into the dark interior of the cave, her back to the entrance.

"Grrrrrr! . . . Grrrrrr!

"Grrrrrr! . . . Grrrrrr!"

In the dim light, Viola first saw an immense creature's glistening, white, curved canine teeth.
Then it's broad forehead.
It's golden eyes.
Thick, gold-colored fur.
Short legs.
"A big cat!" Viola breathed.

Under the big cat's chin, the neck fur had a pearl-white diamond shape that glowed in the dark.

"You are the saber-toothed cat!" Viola exclaimed.

"Grrrrrr! Indeed, I am. And who are you to invade my cave and disturb my day?" said the massive cat.

"I'm Viola, a friend of Don the Pteranodon, who brought me here to stay safe from the storm."

"I eat pteranodons for breakfast, lunch, and dinner, Viola. You might have escaped a bad storm only to face a fierce enemy."

Viola politely asked, "Do you have a name?"

"Grrrrrr! . . . Grrrrrr! . . . Grrrrrr!" With each growl, the beast slowly lifted and lowered its head, stepping closer to Viola. Now, it was only an arm's length away.

"I am Artemio, the Saber-Toothed Cat—a Smilodon and protector of Artemis, the Greek goddess of the hunt, wilderness, wild animals, and the moon."

The beast was now so close to Viola that each time it growled, she could feel its thick, hot breath blow against her face and brush past her cheeks.

Viola watched the animal. With each breath, its broad chest rose and fell. Artemio was a giant creature.

Facing Artemio, Viola saw that her eyes were level with his chin.

She heard his forceful, loud heartbeat, "lub-DUB…lub-DUB…lub-DUB…lub-DUB!"

Artemio demanded, "Tell me why I should not tear you into pieces and devour you right now, Viola."

Survival instinct drove Viola to reach

into her pajama pocket with her right hand, feeling the 6-pack of nail polish and the leather case holding the sharp fabric scissors.

She wondered, "Is that all I have to defend myself?

"No, I also have God, patience, truth, skill, and wisdom on my side."

She asked, "Artemio, you could have devoured me and Don the Pteranodon the moment we landed in your cave. But you didn't. Instead, you waited silently in the dark at the back of the cave until Don left, leaving me alone. Why?"

Artemio remained silent, prompting Viola to take the next step.

Viola was intelligent and naturally strong in body, mind, and spirit.

"Alright, Artemio, I've got a deal for you.

"I carry two powerful tools in my pocket.

"One is a weapon that I can kill you with, instantly." As she said this, she unzipped the leather case protecting her fingers from the sharp scissors and gripped the handle. Viola kept her hand with the scissors hidden in her pocket.

"The other is war paint that can make you look even fiercer to your prey and enemies. And you'll be one drop-dead gorgeous, giant feline for all eternity.

"You can only choose one. Which will you pick?" Viola asked.

Artemio stepped back and waited there. His piercing yellow eyes burned into her. His sharp saber teeth gleamed. His powerful, steely claws dug into the cave's sandy floor. Artemio was ready to attack Viola.

"Maybe I will take both!" Artemio said with a hint of clever mischief.

Viola calmly repeated the words of her bargain. "I said, 'Which one do you choose?'"

Artemio stepped closer to Viola. He briefly glanced at her pocket before locking eyes with her. Then, Artemio paused to assess Viola's physical strength and fighting attitude.

Artemio faced Viola head-on as a fierce opponent, with his knees bent and his back arched for the attack.

He was ready.

"As you wish," he said. "I am Artemio the Saber-Toothed Cat. I resent vanity. I despise those who fight and kill to take spoils.

"And cheat.

"And lie.

"And they are cowards and hypocrites.

"I take only what I need. I do only what I have to.

"I value loyalty, decency, truth, faith, love, and honesty.

"And I treat everyone else as I would want them to treat me and my kind."

Then the giant cat stood perfectly still like a statue.

"I will choose the weapon!" Artemio replied.

Viola took a firm step forward.

Lightning-fast, she pulled the scissors from her pocket in a hammer grip and expertly pressed the steely, razor-sharp tip to Artemio's jugular vein next to the glowing diamond pearl-white spot.

With every heartbeat, Artemio's jugular pulsated strongly beneath the glowing diamond. "lub-DUB…lub-DUB…lub-DUB…lub-DUB!"

Artemio didn't flinch. He waited patiently like all great cats. His fierce, gold eyes looked deeply into Viola's brown eyes.

Viola looked intensely into Artemio's eyes and stayed still.

She waited, standing firm with the scissors tip ready to end the cat's life and save herself. She pressed the razor-sharp scissors slightly against Artemio's jugular vein, prepared to kill him with a single jab if necessary. Her breathing was deep but steady, and her muscles were taut.

Silence.

Time went by.

Artemio said, "Viola, you have a deadly weapon at my throat now. With a slight stab, you could deliver a mortal blow to a beast as mighty and as vicious as I am. Even more impressive, Viola, you are a clever young girl with a spirit and a voice that scream courage, resolve, and fearlessness."

Artemio took two steps back, respectfully bowed his head to the ground, then slowly lifted his head again.

Artemio said, "Viola, you have passed the test of the fittest warrior. I congratulate you. Please undo this gold chain wrapped around my forepaw. It bears a heart-shaped gold pendant engraved with the image of Artemis, the Greek goddess, the lady I'm sworn to protect. Inside the pendant is a lock of hair cut from her head. It is my greatest honor to give this to someone as brave as you."

Viola withdrew the scissors and put them back in the leather case in her pocket.

She grasped the gold chain and pendant with the image and hair

of Artemis, the goddess, held tightly shut by a gold clasp. On the back was engraved, "Viola, you have a calm, nurturing spirit, but when provoked, you will strike fear into the hearts of your enemies."

"Thank you, Artemio," she said. "Such kind words. I will cherish this beautiful gift forever."

Viola slipped the pendant into the pocket of her pajamas with the nail polish and scissors.

"Viola," Artemio continued, "I have the utmost respect for you."

"Most other opponents would have run

from me, and I would have devoured them. Many would have fainted at the sight of an opponent as demanding and monstrous as I am. And I would have devoured them.

"They are the most confused, weak, hopeless, and fickle creatures of all time. They have godless and empty souls. They are unfaithful to themselves and their kind.

"You stood brave and resolute in defending yourself. You remained calm despite a serious threat and imminent death. You chose to follow the righteous path, willing to fight for your life, for your loved ones, and for your sacred beliefs."

Artemio said, "You will win against the enemies of goodness."

Viola heard Don's wings flapping as he arrived at the cave entrance.

She glanced over her shoulder and saw the giant bird land on the sandy ground and skillfully bounce on its two legs.

She turned around to face Artemio, hoping to introduce him to Don.

But Artemio was no longer there.

Don shouted excitedly, "Viola, I love the paint you applied to my claws and beak! My buddies screamed with envy."

Then Don said, "But the storm has passed. The sun is out, and it's now evening. Before it gets dark, we must fly immediately to the place where I picked you up. Harriet, Harold, and Solomon won't be happy if I'm late. Hop on!"

Viola climbed onto Don's back and held onto his neck tightly.

She looked back into the cave where she and Artemio had stood together. She saw their footprints in the sandy floor.

Viola shouted, "Goodbye, Artemio! I will miss you."

"Grrrrrr! . . . Grrrrrr! . . . Grrrrrr!"

Artemio spoke to Viola, but now his words came from deep within her heart.

Farewell, Viola, my friend. I shared timeless truths with you from our God, who:

"Created the human in his image, in the image of God He created him, male and female He created them."

Our God, who comforts us.
Believe in yourself.
Have faith in God.
Pray to God reverently every night.
Love your mother, father, and family.
Always strive to do what is right,
true, and good!
I will be by your side throughout time
to protect you.

Then she heard Don say, "Viola, hold on tight. We must go back to Harold, Harriet, and Solomon now. They are waiting for you, and I'm sure they are worried about your safety."

Don jumped off the edge of the cave, and they fell into the open space below.

Don winged hard, lifting them higher and higher above the ancient land, over the lush forests, valleys, rivers, meadows, and the immense volcano.

Viola asked, "Don, how will you survive in this land of dinosaurs that is so full of dangers?"

Don answered, "Life goes on. We are wild animals, fortunate to wake up every day and have our lives just as they are. We always do our best. And we will keep living. We cannot expect anything more."

Minutes later, they reached the exact spot where Don had pecked Viola's shoulder earlier that morning. From there, they began their journey into the land where all the dinosaurs roam.

"You are later than we expected, Don," Harriet said, scolding him.

"Sorry, Owls, I did my best. There was a bad thunderstorm," Don replied.

Solomon, looking very stern, swooped down from his perch to land on the soft, bent-over grass bed. Viola climbed up his outstretched leg to his shoulders and sat on his neck, as she had before. Then Solomon, Harriet, and Harold soared fiercely into the evening sky.

"So long, Don," Viola said.

Don said, "Good-bye, Viola. Thanks for painting my unguals and beak."

Momma swung open the door to Viola's bedroom and turned on the lamp.

"Click."

Viola was sleeping peacefully in her bed at home, cozy and warm under the covers.

"Good morning, Viola," Momma said, touching her hand. "Hope you slept well."

Viola sat up, rubbed her eyes, and said, "Oh, Momma, I had the most wonderful night ever! You wouldn't believe it."

She rolled over to sit on the edge of her bed. She looked in the pocket of her pajamas for the six-pack of nail polish and the fabric scissors. Then she searched for the chain with the engraved gold pendant and the locket of hair from the Greek goddess Artemis. She wanted to show the locket to Momma.

But her pocket was empty.

"What's wrong?" Momma asked, touching Viola's shoulder where Don the Pteranodon had pecked her in the dream.

Momma saw that Viola looked sad.

Deep in her heart, Viola recalled the last words Artemis said:

Farewell, Viola, my friend. I shared timeless truths with you from our God, who:

"Created the human in his image, in the image of God He created him, male and female He created them."

Our God, who comforts us.
Believe in yourself.
Have faith in God.
Pray to God reverently every night.
Love your mother, father, and family.
Always strive to do what is right, true, and good!
I will be by your side throughout time to protect you.

"I'm okay, Momma," Viola answered sleepily.

"I had a dream where I met the most wonderful friend, Artemio. He taught me about all the important things in life.

"Momma, I feel so lucky to have you and Daddy as my parents.

"I love you and Daddy so much."

A note to parents, guardians, and teachers:

This little story, *Artemio's Gift*, takes a young girl, Viola, on a fun time-travel adventure back to the land where dinosaurs roamed. After seeing many different dinosaurs in their natural environment, Viola escapes a terrible storm and waits it out in the safety of a cave. An enormous sabertooth cat, Artemio, comes to her from far back in the cave and challenges Viola. She meets every challenge. Artemio awards her with a gold pendant. He also shares with Viola the virtues of living a good life.

Mario Lampic created the images and book design for *Artemio* to entertain and create enthusiasm among readers from the first sentence to the last.

Stories are magical for young and old alike. Children are naturally incredibly imaginative and voracious learners. So, feed their appetites day in and day out, until they fall fast asleep for a nap, or at day's end.

This is your opportunity to guide your child into the beautiful world of literature and the joy of lifelong learning. The journey starts now. You will treasure and never forget the time you spend teaching your child to read and to love learning.

Best wishes!

Charles Bruckerhoff

is the publisher of

 Sequoia House Books™

and author of

Juliet's I'm a Girl and I Know Things: A Children's Book Series,

Adelyn's Adventure Series,

and an adult novel,

Plowman: Harvest of Grain and Innocence.

He gardens, bakes bread, cooks, and studies American history, ancient civilizations of the world, the Hebrew Bible, and the Saint John's Bible. He loves to spend time with his wife and family. He places no limit on new adventures.

Did you find places where *Peabody* was hiding?

(Here are the solutions!)

www.ingramcontent.com/pod-product-compliance
Lightning Source LLC
Chambersburg PA
CBRC101143030426
42337CB00008B/64

When you're not feeling well, slow down and play a game or two of tic-tac-toe.

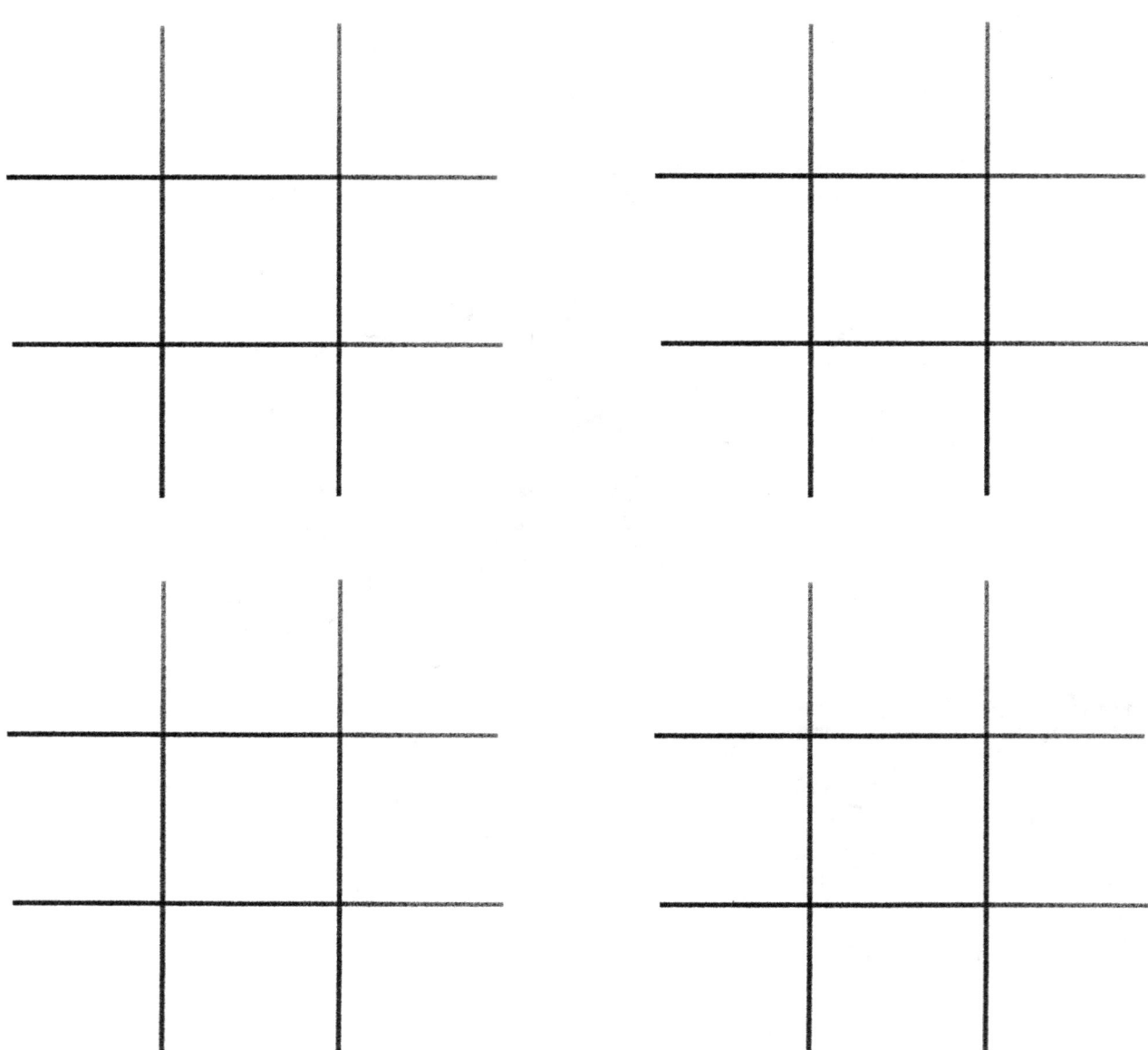

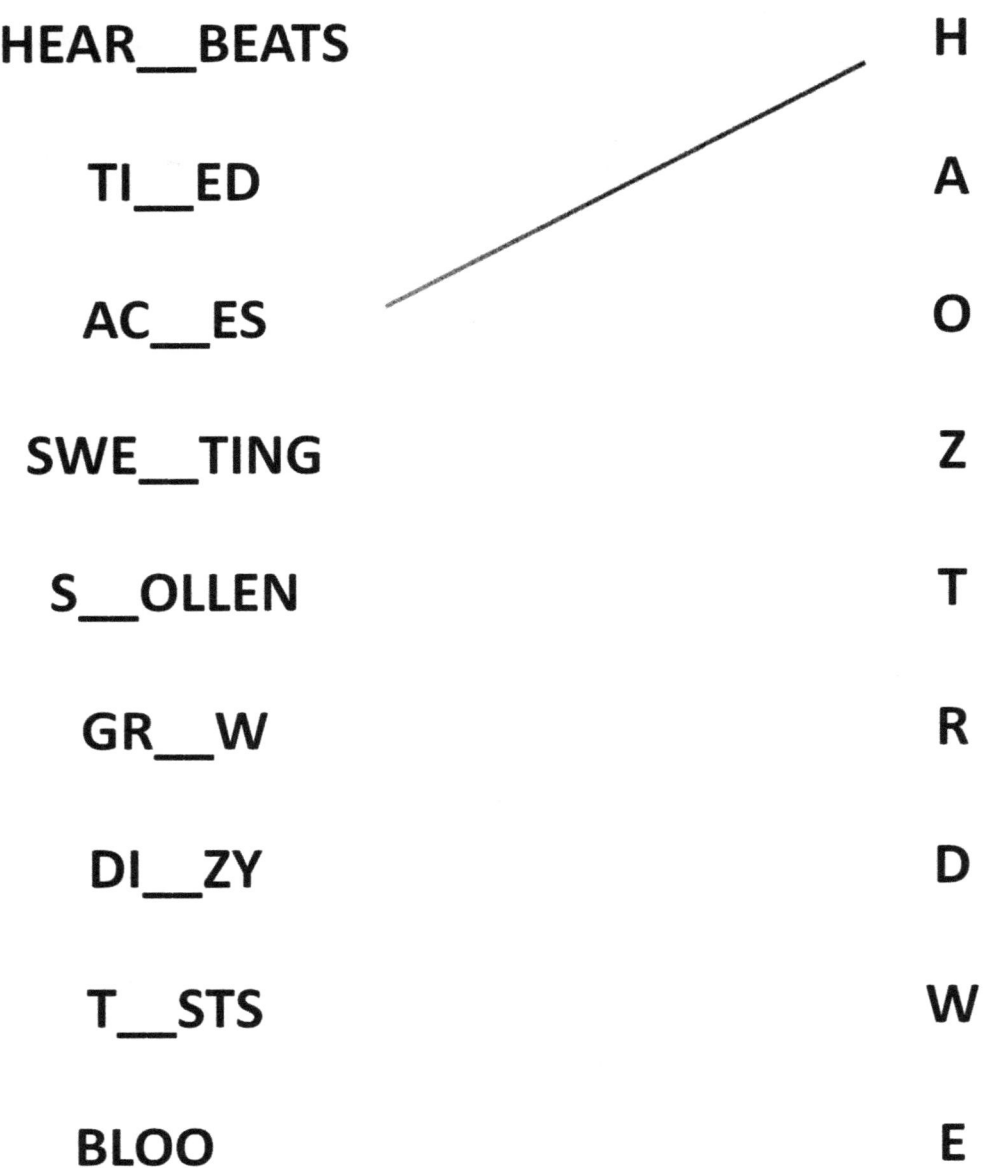

Word Search

```
C S C G R T K Z E B
S H W J A O A H Z L
W T E O E R C D C O
E C I S L A H J D O
A E V R T L M I D D
T A C S E X E S I D
Y M E H N D R N Z R
H H W H O L F A Z A
C B R E A T H T Y W
E C G R O W I N G Z
```

TIRED   BREATH   CHESTACHE   SWEATY

SWOLLEN   DIZZY   GROWING

ECG   ECHO   CHESTXRAY   BLOODDRAW

The electrocardiogram (ECG) looks at (choose 1 answer):

A) the heart's electrical activities
B) the bones
C) how the blood flows in and out of the heart

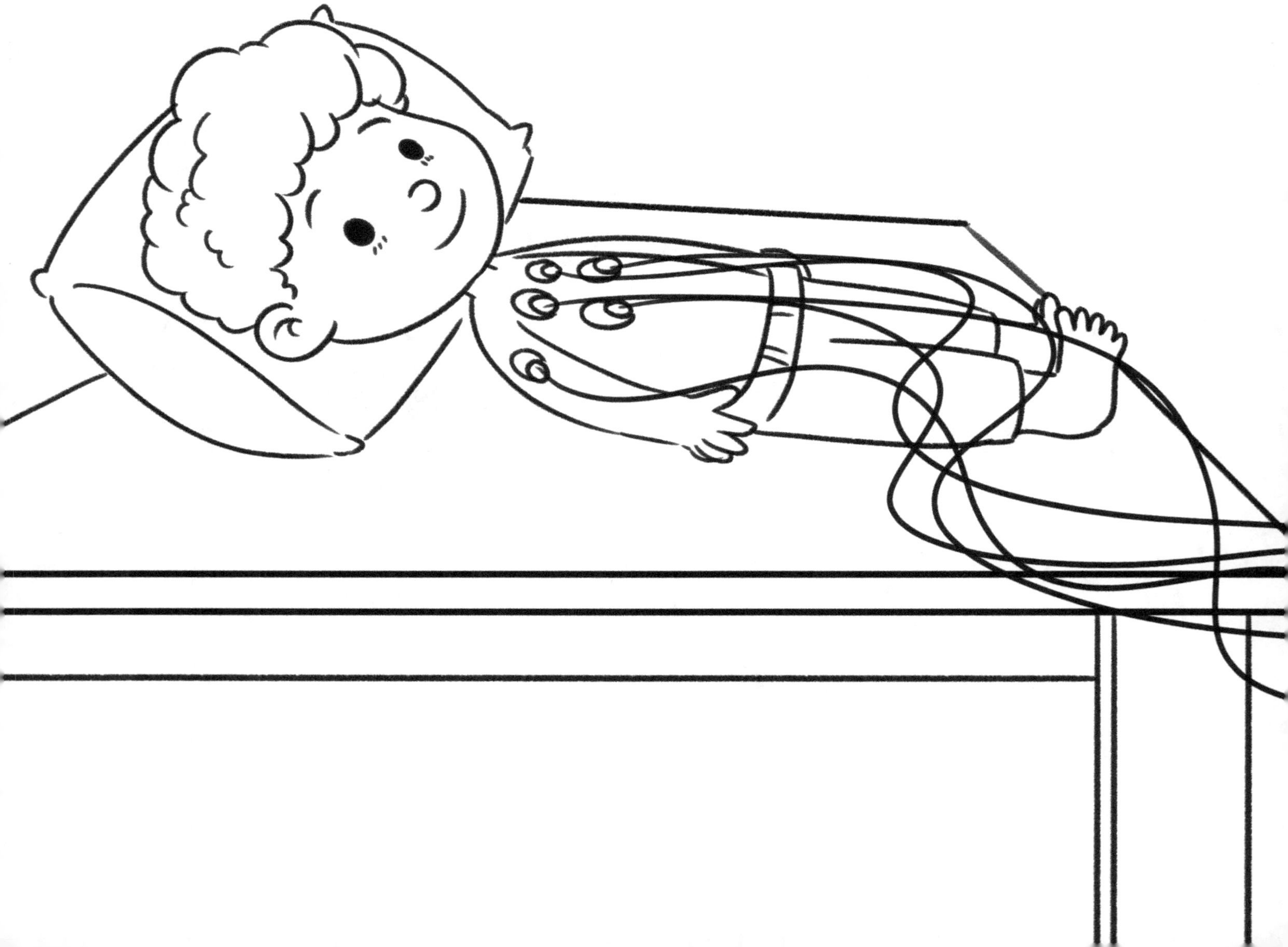

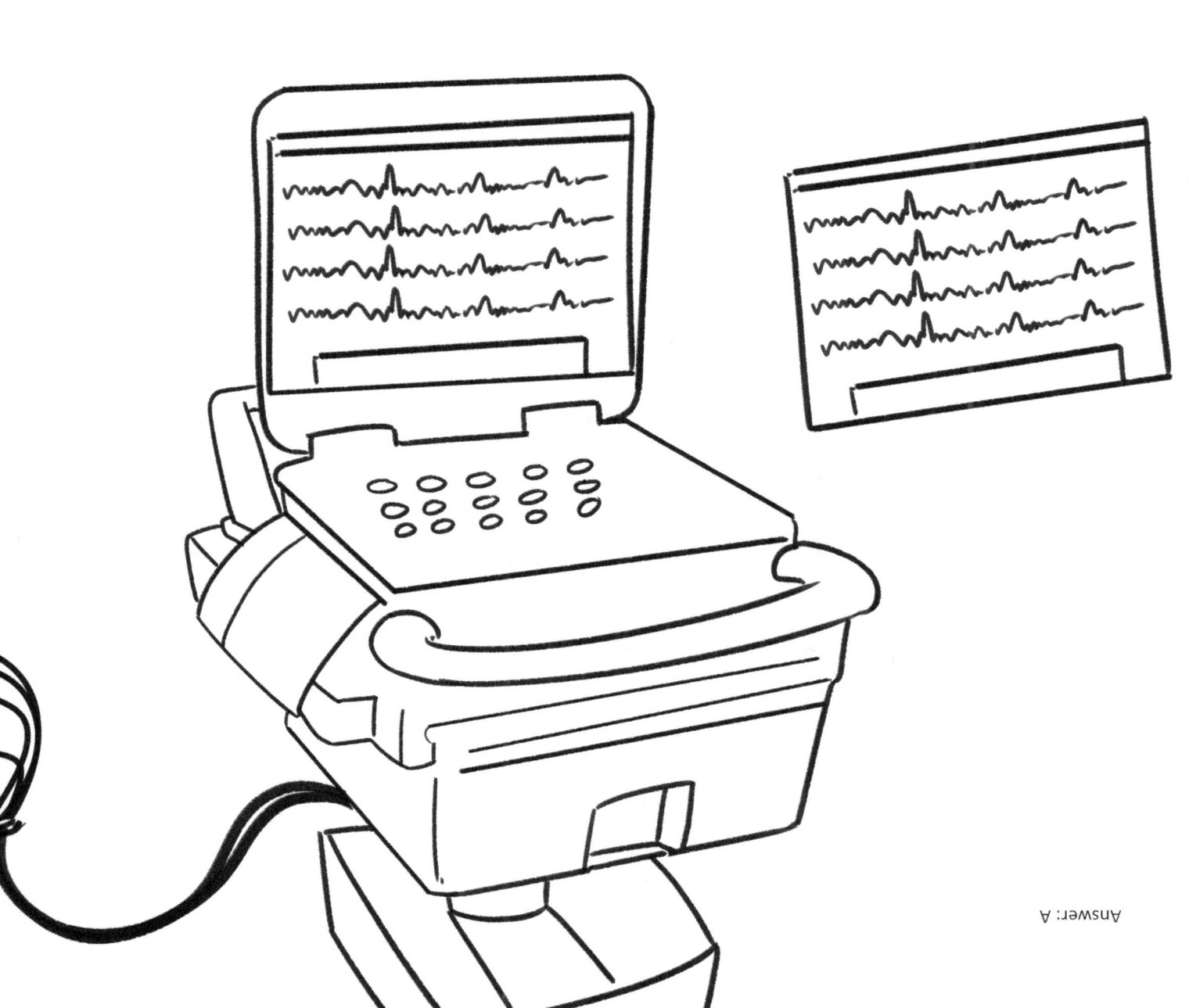

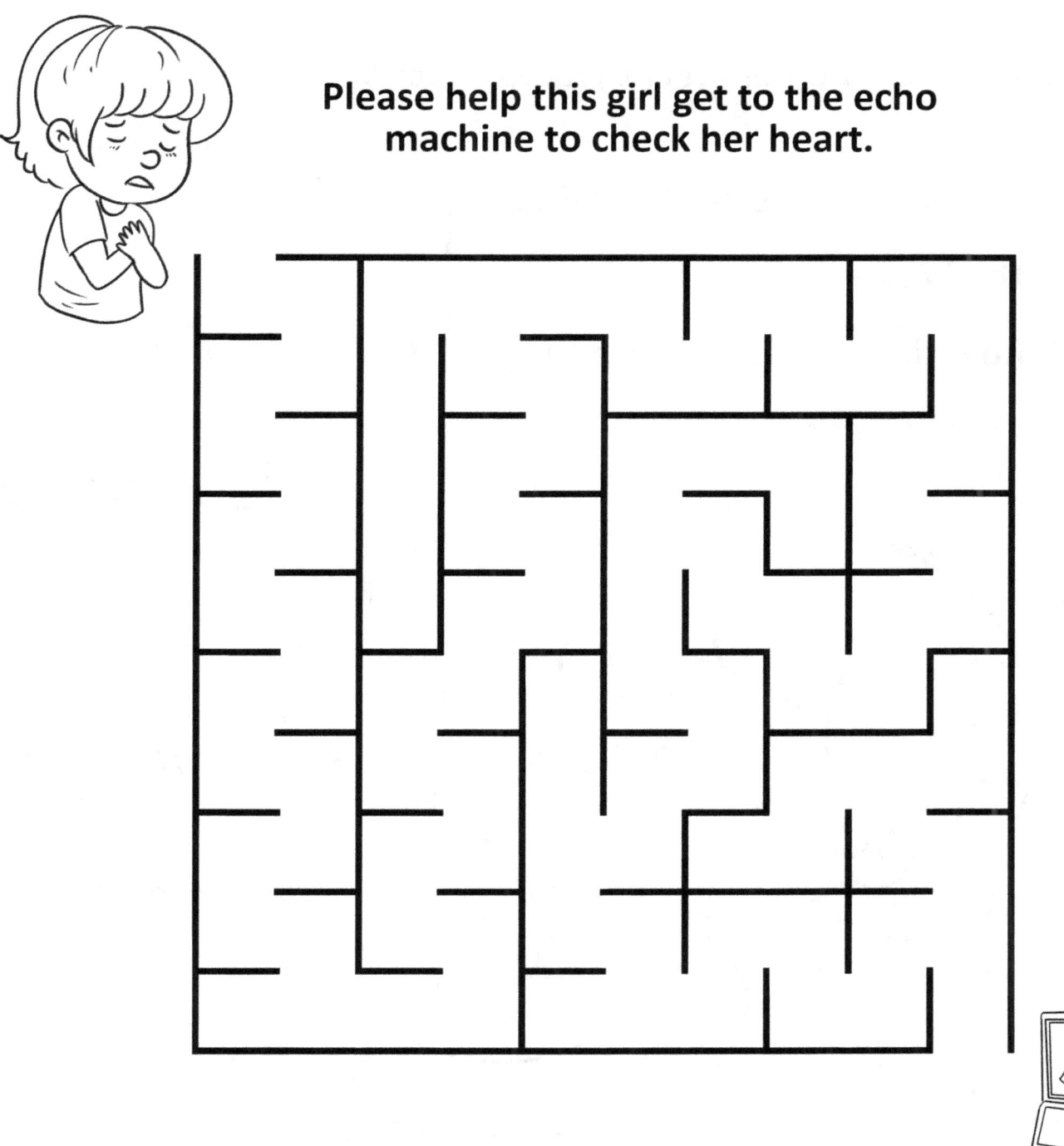

The echocardiogram (echo) looks at (choose 1 answer):

A) the heart's electrical activities

B) the bones

C) how the blood flows in and out of the heart

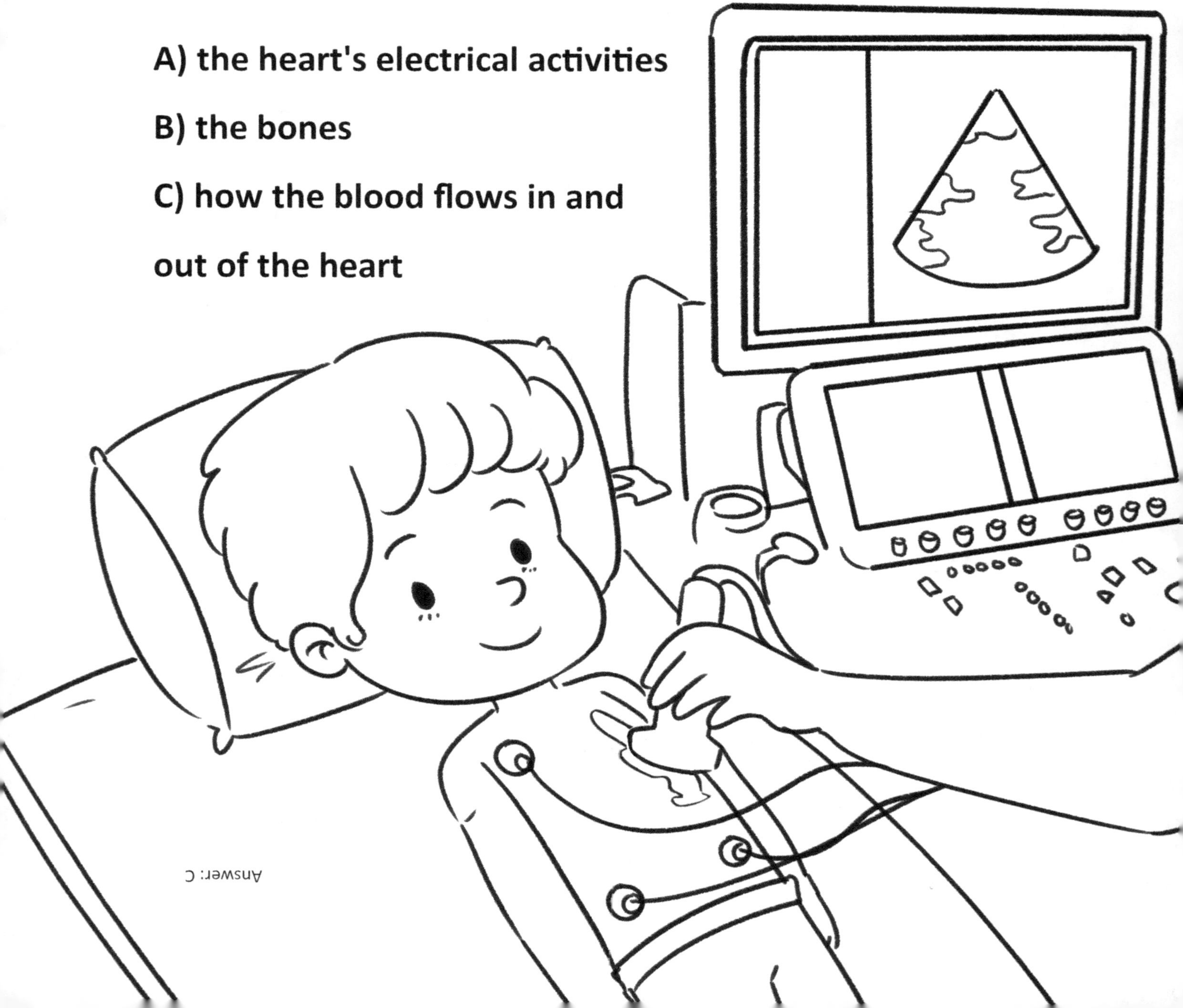

Answer: C

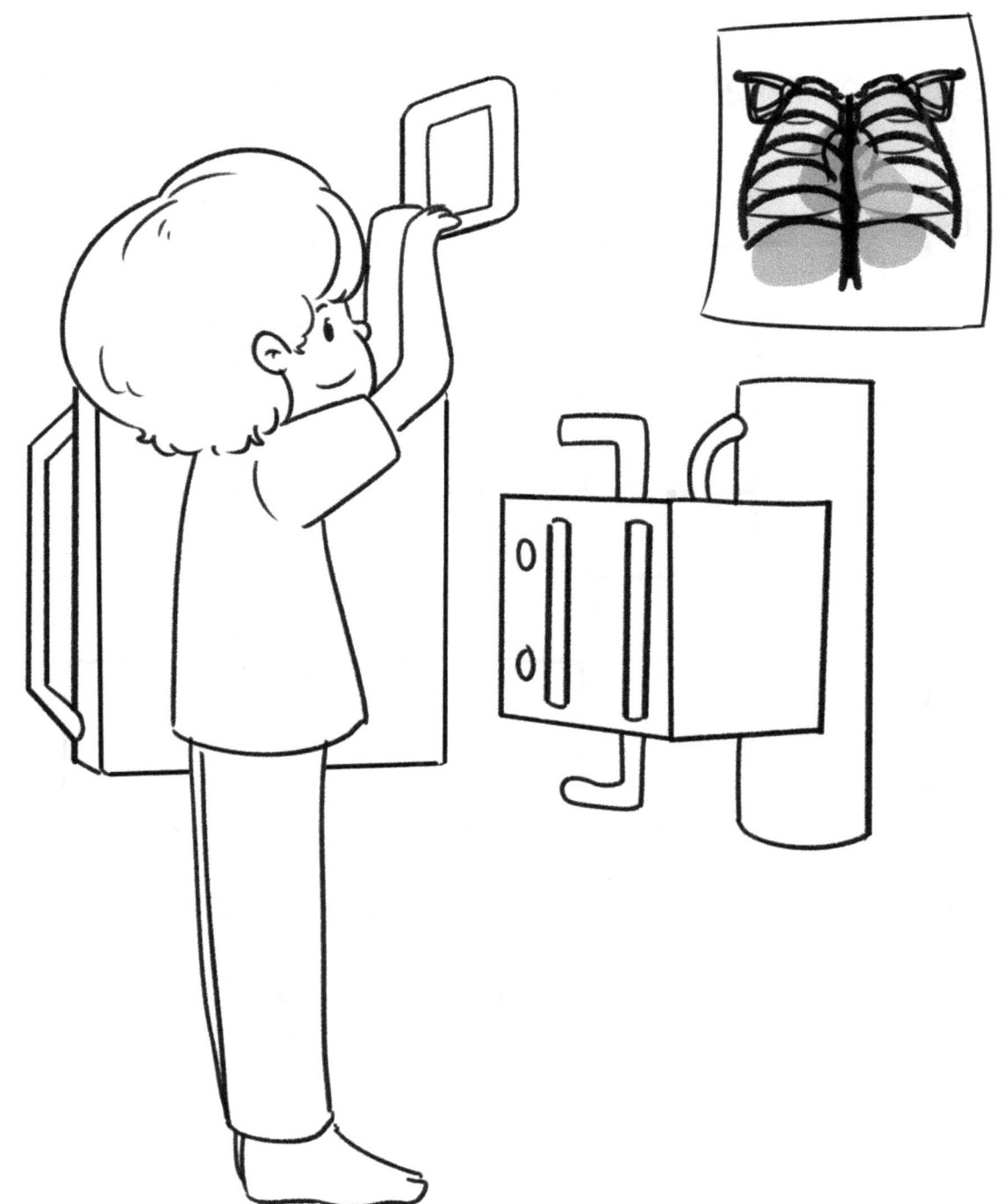

Please help this boy get to his blood draw.

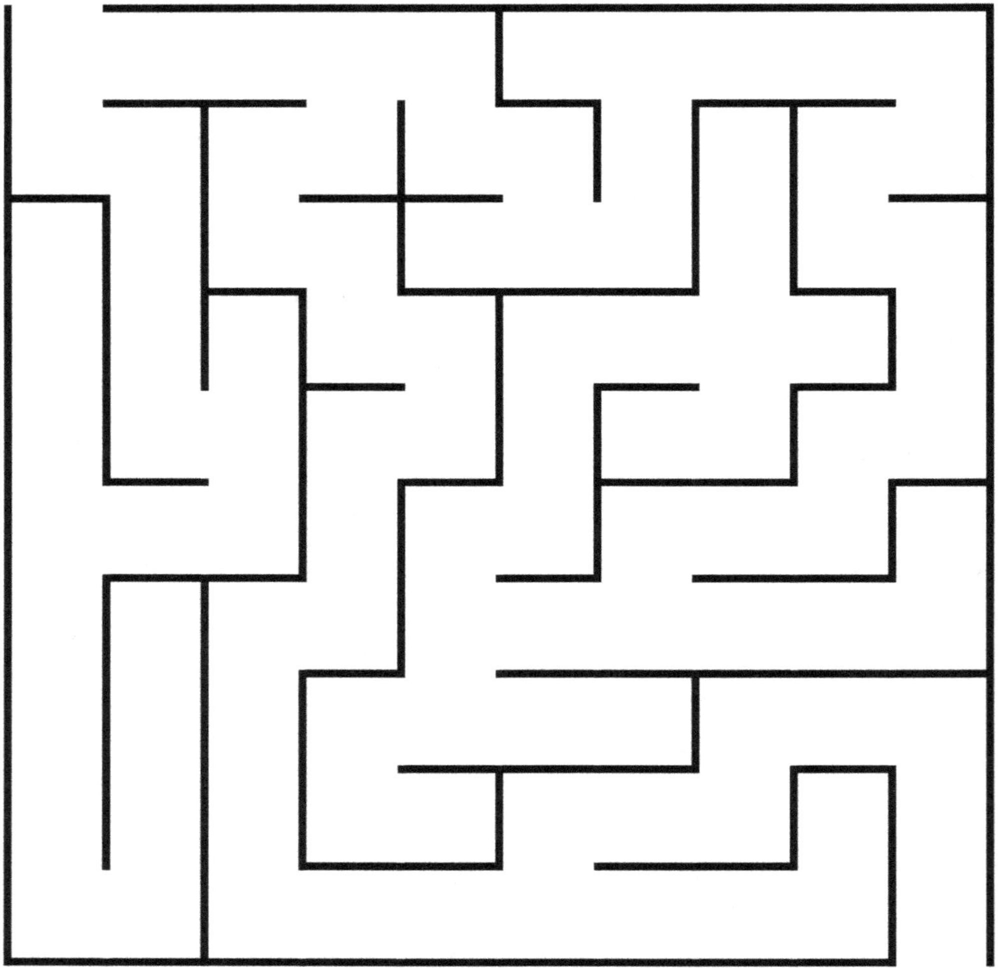

Please help this boy get to the chest X-ray.

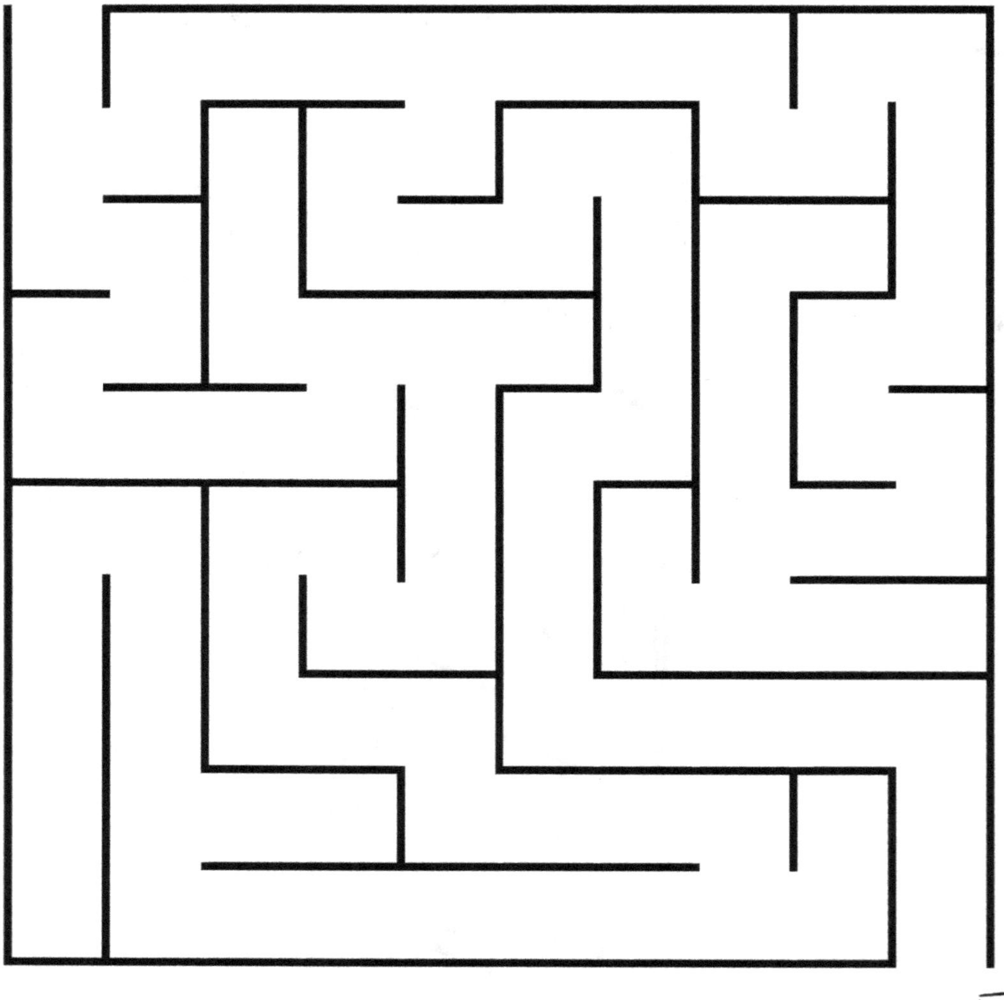

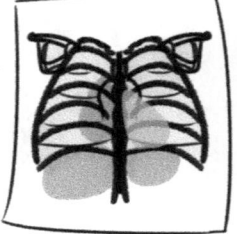

Word Search

```
L S C D S C A R D H
B O A O R Z O T B R
I E U F M E C L T E
E N T E E F A M R C
F G P T Y D O M D O
C A T H E T E R S V
W I S B F R S L T E
U S T R O N G E R R
D Q S U R G E R Y Y
R Y T U B E S E Q I
```

SURGERY   DREAM   SAFE

COMFORT   TUBES   CATHETERS   SCAR

RECOVERY   BETTER   STRONGER

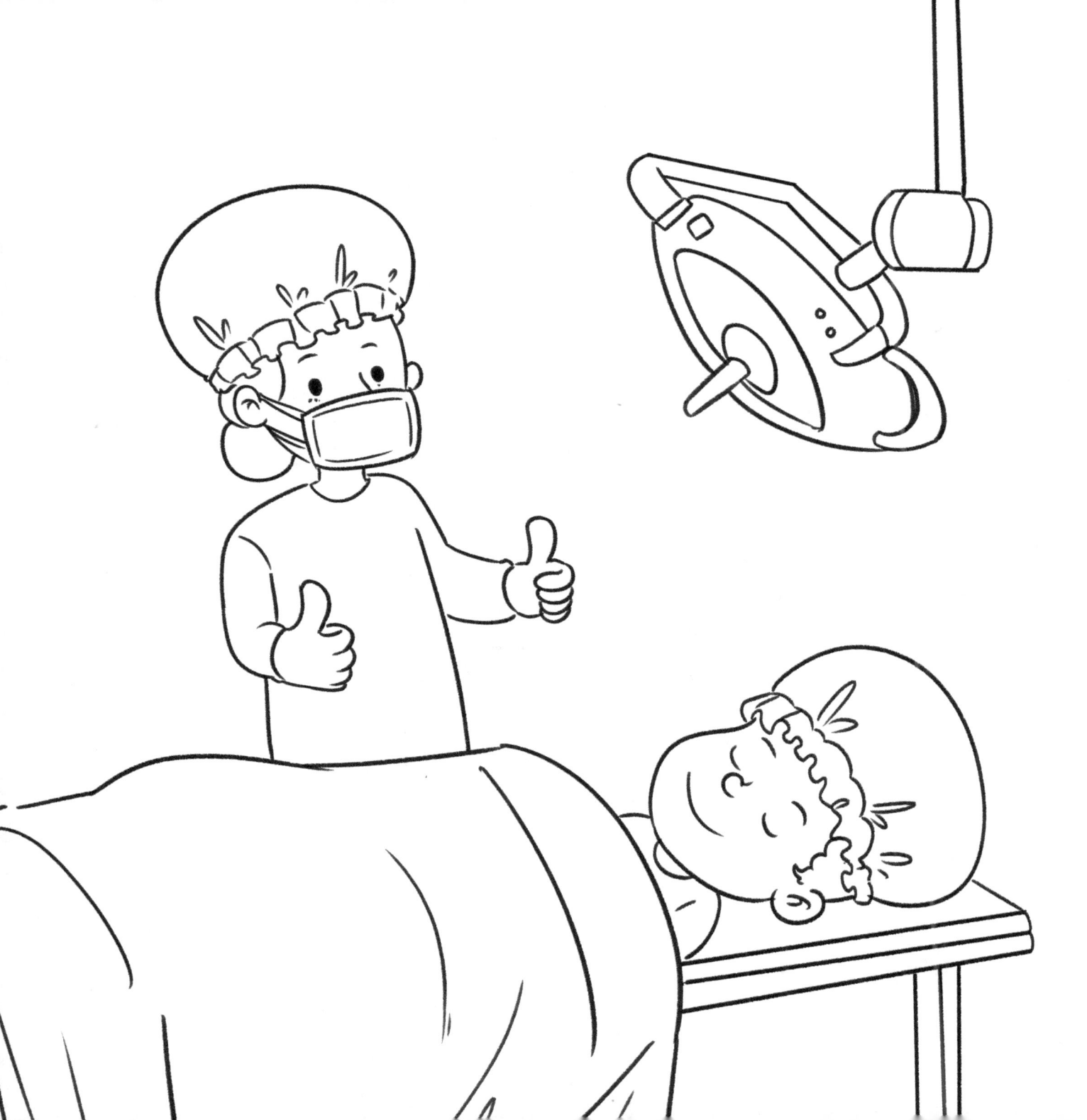

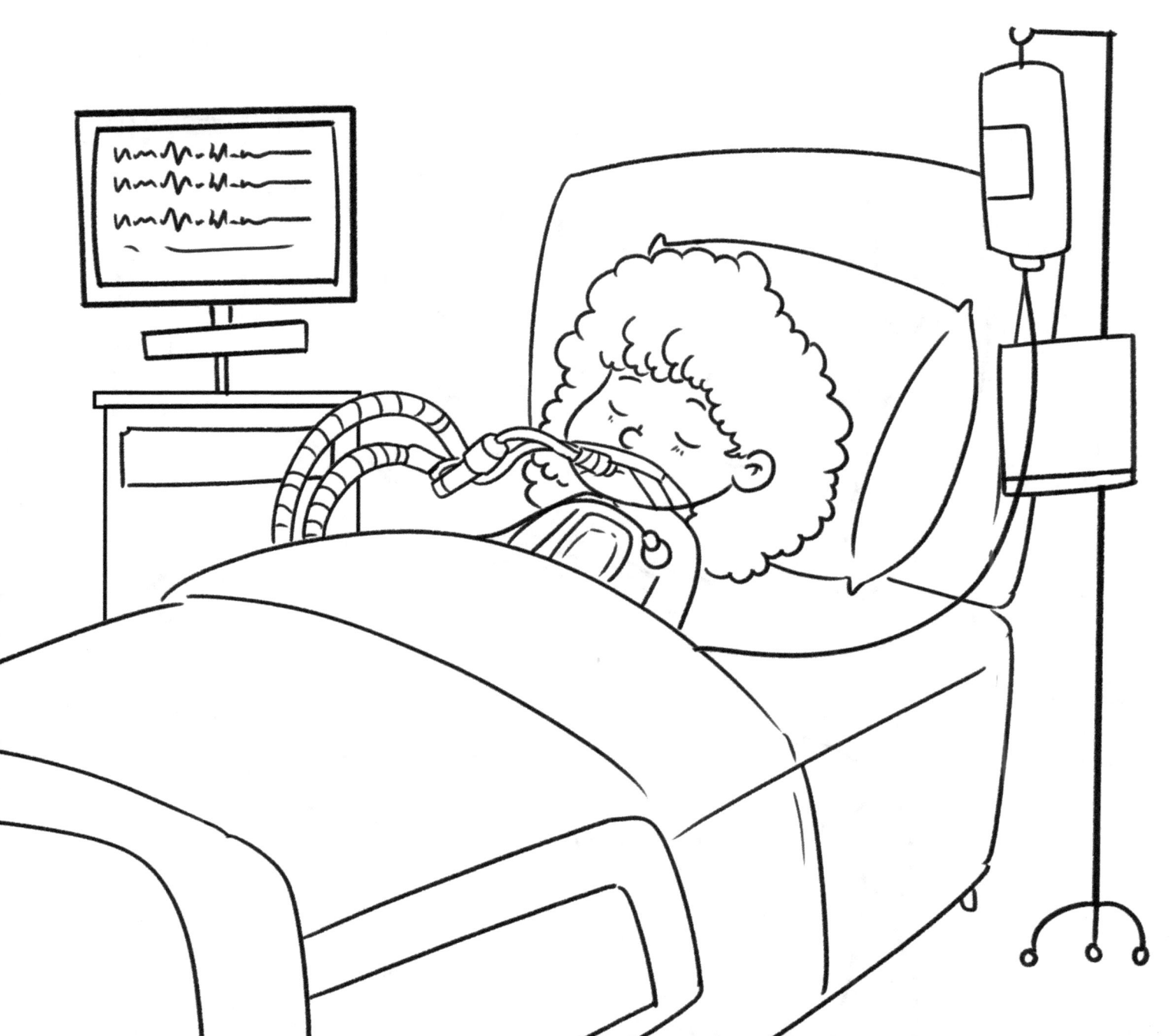

Word Search

```
U R S B I S U C I W
B E U E L U W O X O
R S R A S P A U F R
A I V U S E R R I T
V L I T T R R A G H
E I V I R H I G H Y
N E O F O E O E T A
T N R U N R R O E C
T T J L G O T U R X
L O V E D Y D S C V
```

COURAGEOUS   BRAVE   WORTHY   LOVED

BEAUTIFUL   STRONG   RESILIENT   SURVIVOR

FIGHTER   WARRIOR   SUPERHERO

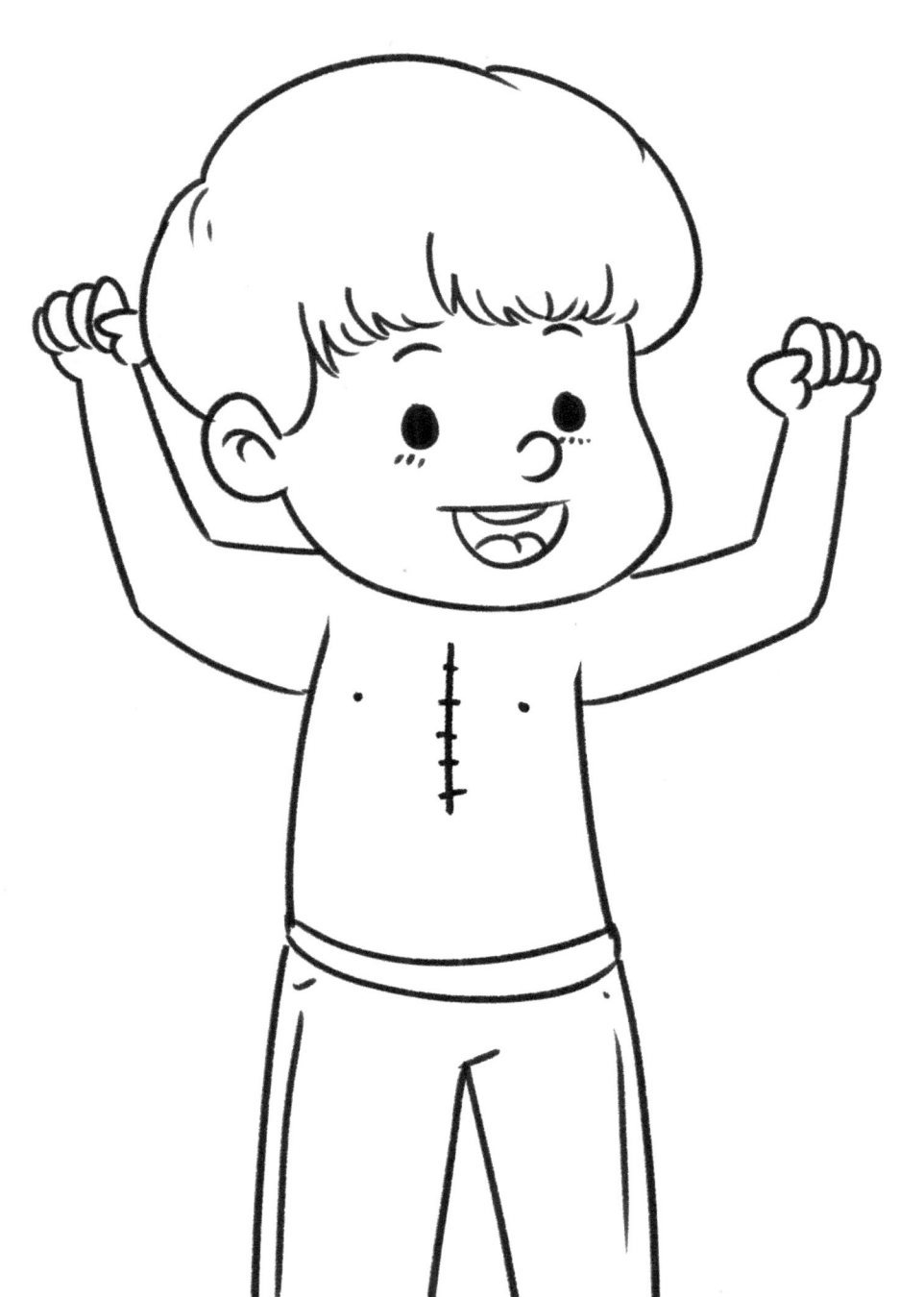

I am

BRAVE

COURAGEOUS

STRONG

CONFIDENT

READY

www.ingramcontent.com/pod-product-compliance
Lightning Source LLC
Chambersburg PA
CBHW080947050426
42337CB00055B/4729